M000004712

DAY HIKES IN THE
BEARTOOTH MOUNTAINS

RED LODGE, MONTANA TO
YELLOWSTONE NATIONAL PARK

by Robert Stone

Photographs by Robert Stone
Published by:
Day Hike Books, Inc.
114 South Hauser Box 865
Red Lodge, MT 59068
Layout & Design: Paula Doherty
Copyright 1997
Library of Congress Catalog Card Number: 96-96513

Distributed by:
ICS Books, Inc.
1370 E. 86th Place
Merrillville, IN 46410
1-800-541-7323
Fax 1-800-336-8334

TABLE OF CONTENTS

THE HIKES

About the Hikes

The Day Hikes Guide to the Beartooth Mountains focuses on scenic day hikes of various lengths. All of the hikes are between the western town of Red Lodge and the northeast entrance to Yellowstone National Park. My goal is to share these hikes with you and others, providing visitors as well as locals easy access to the backcountry.

The road which links Red Lodge, Montana, to Yellowstone Park is the scenic Beartooth Highway. This is the major access road to the hikes found in this book. The dramatic Beartooth Highway, or Highway 212, begins in Red Lodge, Montana, passes through Cooke City and Silver Gate, and extends to the northeast entrance of Yellowstone National Park. Once inside the park, the road follows a canyon into the Lamar Valley, an elk and bison winter range.

The 68-mile Beartooth Highway was originally built in 1936. It has since been designated a National Scenic Byway and heralded as "the most scenic highway in America" by Charles Kuralt of CBS News. Although the highway starts and ends in Montana, it crosses into Wyoming along the way (map on page 6). The highway is open, weather permitting, Memorial Day through mid-October.

The three-billion year old Absaroka-Beartooth Mountains, which include the Gallatin, Custer, and Shoshone National Forests, surround the Beartooth Highway. These ancient mountains are among the oldest rocks on earth and lie within a 945,000-acre protected wilderness area. The Beartooth Plateau, shaped by alpine glaciers, is the largest continuous area above 10,000 feet and the largest alpine tundra region in North America. There are 27 peaks rising more than 12,000 feet. Granite Peak, the highest peak in Montana, sits at 12,799 feet within this mountain range. These rugged, majestic mountains contain glaciers, deep canyons, streams, waterfalls, more than a thousand lakes, vast alpine meadows, lush forests, abundant wildlife, and sixteen forest service campgrounds. The famous

Beartooth Highway switchbacks start along the east wall of Rock Creek Canyon at 6,000 feet and quickly rise to a top-of-the-world elevation of 10,947 feet. The views from this area are spectacular. The Beartooth Mountains also contain some of the best trout fishing in the United States. Depending on where you fish, you will need to have the correct state fishing license. Licences may be purchased in Red Lodge, Cooke City, Silver Gate, or the Top of the World Store on the pass.

Red Lodge, originally a mining town settled by Europeans, is now an active resort and ski town that still maintains its western heritage. Buildings preserving the 1800s architecture of brick and sandstone line the main street.

Sixty-four miles southwest of Red Lodge are the old-west mining towns of Cooke City and Silver Gate, located four miles and one mile respectively from Yellowstone National Park.

All of the hikes listed in this guide require easy to moderate effort, unless otherwise noted, and are timed at a leisurely rate. The hikes are visually detailed on Rocky Mountain Surveys and the United States Geographic Survey topographic maps that are listed with each hike. The maps can be purchased at most area sporting goods stores.

As for attire and equipment, tennis shoes, as opposed to hiking boots, are fine for any of these hikes. The elevation of the hikes can be as high as 10,000 feet. At this altitude, the air can be cool. Afternoon thundershowers are common throughout the summer. Be prepared for unpredictable weather by wearing layered clothing and a warm hat. A rain poncho, sunscreen, mosquito repellent, and drinking water are also recommended. Pack a lunch and enjoy a picnic at scenic outlooks, streams, or wherever you find the best spot.

Enjoy your hike!

NOTE: A bear bell is advised to alert bears of your presence. The Beartooth Mountains have both black and grizzly bears.

BEARTOOTH
MOUNTAINS

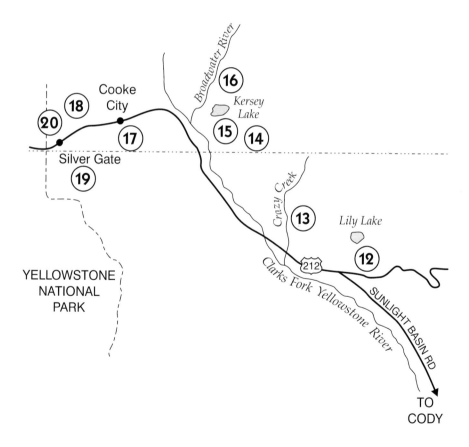

N
W   E
S

Cooke
City

18

20

17

Silver Gate

19

Broadwater River

16

Kersey
Lake

15   14

Crazy Creek

13

Lily Lake

12

212

YELLOWSTONE
NATIONAL
PARK

Clarks Fork Yellowstone River

SUNLIGHT BASIN RD

TO
CODY

MAP OF

RED LODGE MOUNTAIN
SKI AREA

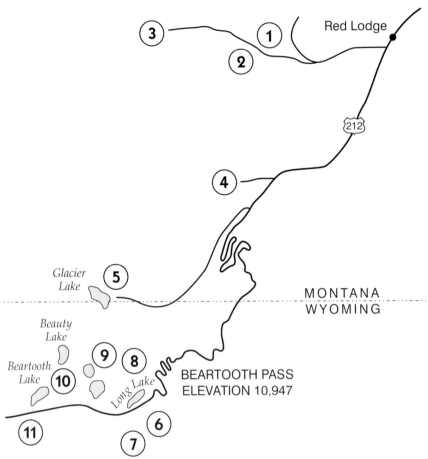

THE HIKES

Hike 1
Wild Bill Lake

Hiking distance: 0.8 mile loop
Hiking time: 30 minutes
Elevation gain: Level hiking
Topo: R.M.S. Alpine-Mount Maurice
 U.S.G.S. Red Lodge West

Summary of hike: Wild Bill Lake was created in a natural glacial depression by "Wild Bill" Kurtzer in 1902. Wild Bill stocked the lake and rented boats as a commercial venture.

This trail circles the perimeter of the lake. There are two fishing docks extending out into the lake with sitting benches (photo on page 31). One dock is located at the end of the peninsula. A picnic area with tables sits among the lodgepole pines on the east side of the lake by the parking lot. Wild Bill Lake is popular as a children's fishing area and is also wheelchair accessible.

Driving directions: Wild Bill Lake is located 6 miles from Red Lodge. Take Highway 212 to the south end of Red Lodge. Turn right (west) onto the road to Red Lodge Mountain ski area. At 2.8 miles, go to the left, turning onto West Fork Road. Continue 3.3 miles further to the Wild Bill Lake parking area on the right. Turn right and park.

Hiking directions: From the parking lot, walk north, past the restrooms, up to the bridge that crosses the lake spillway. The trail curves left to a Y-junction. The left fork leads to the peninsula. The right fork continues around the lake and back to the parking lot.

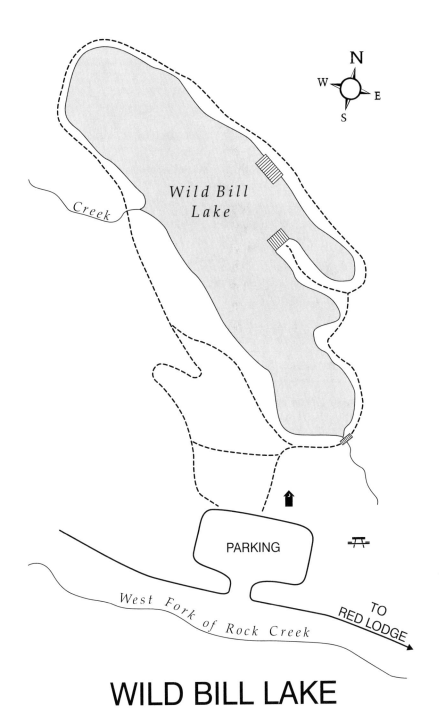

WILD BILL LAKE

Hike 2
Basin Lakes Trail

Hiking distance: 8 miles round trip
Hiking time: 5 hours
Elevation gain: 1,200 feet
Topo: R.M.S. Alpine-Mount Maurice
U.S.G.S. Bare Mountain

Summary of hike: The trail to Lower and Upper Basin Lakes is a gradual but steady uphill climb along a beautiful cascading stream. It passes a waterfall early on. The trail winds through evergreen forests and includes two log creek crossings. Lower Basin Lake has an abundance of lily pads and is very picturesque. Upper Basin Lake is at the base of a majestic mountain bowl, with its snow melt emptying into the lake.

Driving directions: The Basin Creek trailhead is located 7 miles from Red Lodge. Take Highway 212 to the south end of Red Lodge. Turn right (west) onto the road to Red Lodge Mountain ski area. At 2.8 miles, go to the left, turning onto West Fork Road. Continue 4.2 miles further to the trailhead parking lot on the left. Turn left and park.

Hiking directions: From the parking lot, the trail heads uphill to the south. The waterfall is 0.4 miles from the trailhead. As the trail curves to the right, climb some boulders along a spur trail to the left to view the two-tier waterfall. A short distance after the falls, the trail parallels Basin Creek to a log crossing over the creek. Continue following the well-defined trail that leads to both lakes. It is approximately 2.5 miles to Lower Basin Lake and 4 miles to Upper Basin Lake. Return along the same trail.

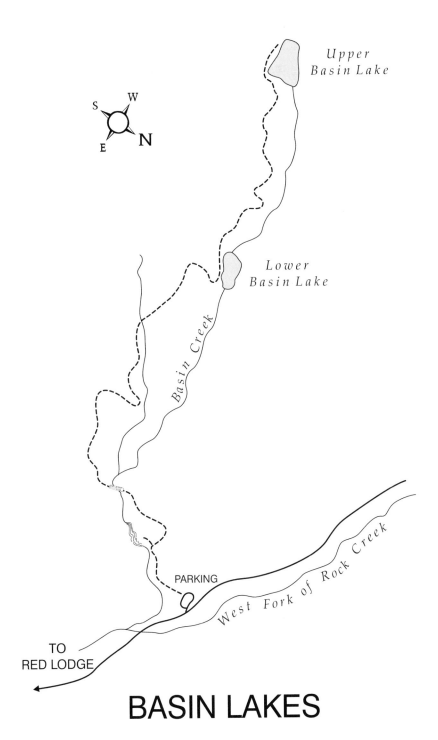

Upper
Basin Lake

Lower
Basin Lake

Basin Creek

West Fork of Rock Creek

PARKING

TO
RED LODGE

BASIN LAKES

Hike 3
West Fork of Rock Creek

Hiking distances:
    3 miles round trip to Calamity Falls: 1.5 hours
    5 miles round trip to Sentinel Falls: 2.5 hours
    8 miles round trip to Quinnebaugh Meadows: 4 hours
    10 miles round trip to Lake Mary: 5 hours
Elevation gain: 350 feet
Topo: R.M.S. Alpine-Mount Maurice
         U.S.G.S. Sylvan Peak, Bare Mountain

Summary of hike: The roaring sounds of the West Fork are always nearby on this hike. Various trickling brooks flow close to the path. The trail winds through the forest and open boulder fields that overlook Rock Creek and the sculptured peaks of Elk and Bowback Mountains. It passes two magnificent waterfalls cutting through rock canyon walls. Both are good lunch spots, with flat rocks for seating. This trail is part of the 19-mile loop that crosses Sundance Pass and ends at the Lake Fork of Rock Creek (Hike 4).

Driving directions: The trailhead is located 13 miles from Red Lodge. Take Highway 212 to the south end of Red Lodge. Turn right (west) onto the road to Red Lodge Mountain ski area. At 2.8 miles, go to the left onto West Fork Road. Continue 10 miles to the trailhead at the end of the road and park.

Hiking directions: Take the trail on the north side of the parking area. It is well maintained and easy to follow. The trail passes several boulder fields enroute to Calamity Falls, about 1.5 miles. The waterfall is not visible from the trail. Listen for the sound of the falls and watch for a side trail on the left that leads to the falls. Sentinel Falls is one mile further along the main trail. This falls is easy to spot and enjoy from the trail. Above Sentinel Falls, the creek opens up to a beautiful, wide, shallow body of water. Quinnebaugh Meadows is one mile further. From the meadow, you may take a side trip to Lake Mary, a steep, uphill one-mile hike. To return, retrace your steps.

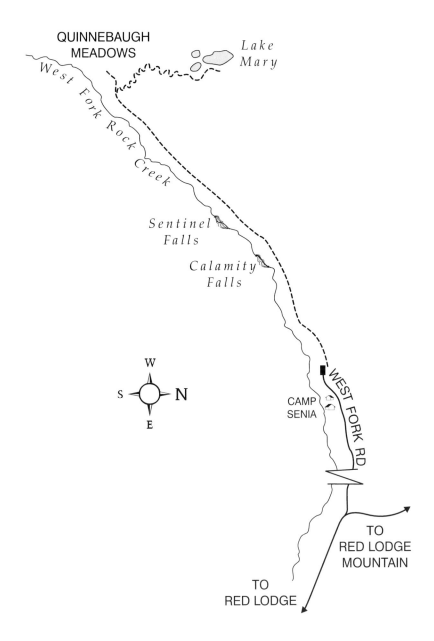

WEST FORK OF
ROCK CREEK

Hike 4
Lake Fork Trail

Hiking distance: 10 miles round trip
Hiking time: 2.5 hours
Elevation gain: 600 feet
Topo: R.M.S. Alpine–Mount Maurice
U.S.G.S. Black Pyramid Mountain, Silver Run Peak

Summary of hike: Located in Lake Fork Canyon, the Lake Fork trail follows a beautiful mountain creek through a lodge-pole pine forest to a series of lakes. Silver Falls, a long, thin waterfall, can be seen flowing down the mountain on the left. Lake Fork is a popular cross-country ski area in the winter.

Driving directions: From Red Lodge, drive 9 miles south on Highway 212 toward the switchbacks to mile marker 59. Turn right at the Lake Fork Road—a sign marks the turn. Drive 2 miles to the end of the road. Park in the trailhead parking lot.

Hiking directions: The trailhead begins at the end of the parking lot. Cross the bridge over Lake Fork and turn right, heading up canyon. The first lake, Lost Lake, is 5 miles up, making for a 10-mile round trip. This area is so beautiful that if you choose not to hike all the way up to the lake, the hike will still be a wonderful experience. Keyser Brown Lake, 2 miles past Lost Lake, is a 14-mile round trip. The trail leading to September Morn Lake is part of a 19-mile trail that crosses Sundance Pass and ends at the West Fork of Rock Creek (Hike 3).

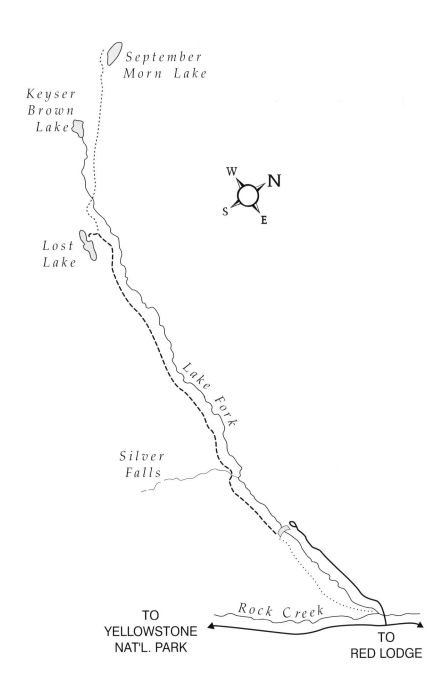

September
Morn Lake

Keyser
Brown
Lake

Lost
Lake

Lake Fork

Silver
Falls

W N
S E

Rock Creek

TO
YELLOWSTONE
NAT'L. PARK

TO
RED LODGE

LAKE FORK TRAIL

Hike 5
Glacier Lake

Hiking distance: 4 miles round trip
Hiking time: 3 hours
Elevation gain: 1,000 feet
Topo: R.M.S. Alpine-Mount Maurice
U.S.G.S. Silver Run Peak

Summary of hike: The trail to Glacier Lake is located at the head of Rock Creek Canyon at an elevation of 9,700 feet. It is a steady, uphill climb to Glacier Lake, the headwaters of Rock Creek. Most of the hike follows the swift, cascading creek with stunning views overlooking the glacial canyon. Take time to look at the rock formations and fascinating, twisted old trees. A wooden bridge crosses Moon Creek a half mile into the hike.

Driving directions: From Red Lodge, take Highway 212 south about 10 miles. Drive 1.5 miles past the Lake Fork Road turnoff, or 0.5 miles past mile marker 58, to a turnoff on the right (west) marked with a campground sign. Turn right and go straight past the campgrounds until the road makes a "T," about 1/2 mile. Turn left and drive 7 miles to the parking lot at the end of the road. The road does get rocky as it nears the trailhead.

Hiking directions: Walk to the end of the parking lot to the trailhead. This well-defined trail leads to Glacier Lake, crossing a bridge over the creek at 0.5 miles. The trail climbs to a ridge that is higher than the lake. From the ridge is a view of the entire lake surrounded by mountains. The trail then descends to the northeastern shoreline. Return along the same trail. (Late spring snows may cover parts of the trail at its higher elevations.)

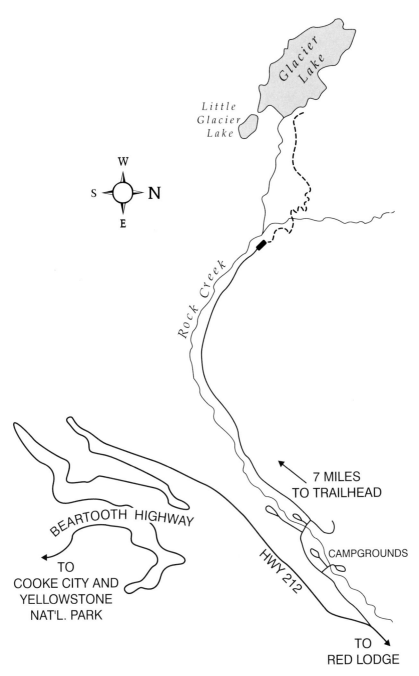

Glacier Lake

Little Glacier Lake

Rock Creek

W **N** **S** **E**

7 MILES
TO TRAILHEAD

BEARTOOTH HIGHWAY

TO
COOKE CITY AND
YELLOWSTONE
NAT'L. PARK

HWY 212

CAMPGROUNDS

TO
RED LODGE

GLACIER LAKE

Hike 6
Hauser, Solar, Fort
and Rainbow Lakes Loop

Hiking distance: 4 miles round trip
Hiking time: 2 hours
Elevation gain: 300 feet
Topo: R.M.S. Wyoming Beartooths
U.S.G.S. Deep Lake

Summary of hike: This loop is a short, easy family hike. It can be walked in under two hours, although it is worth lingering at each of the four lakes. The panoramic views and magic of this area encourage exploration. Various streams trickle over rocks and form pools. Wildflowers are abundant.

Driving directions: Take Highway 212 to Long Lake, 36.5 miles from Red Lodge and 28 miles from Cooke City. Park along the highway pullout at Long Lake (photo on page 26). Across the road to the south is a sign that reads "Hauser Lake Trailhead."

Hiking directions: Start at the "Hauser Lake Trailhead" sign. Walk south, following the cairns (man-made rock mounds used as trail markers). The trail will lead a half mile to Hauser Lake. From here on, there will not be a trail, but you can easily see your way along the rolling, open tundra. Follow the creek flowing out of Hauser Lake, which leads to Solar Lake, a half mile past Hauser Lake. From Solar Lake, hike another half mile due west over the hill to Fort Lake. It will take about 15 minutes. You will not be able to see Fort Lake until you reach the top of the hill. Walk around Fort Lake to the right and head north to Rainbow Lake. From here, continue again to the north. The meadow will lead you back to the trailhead.

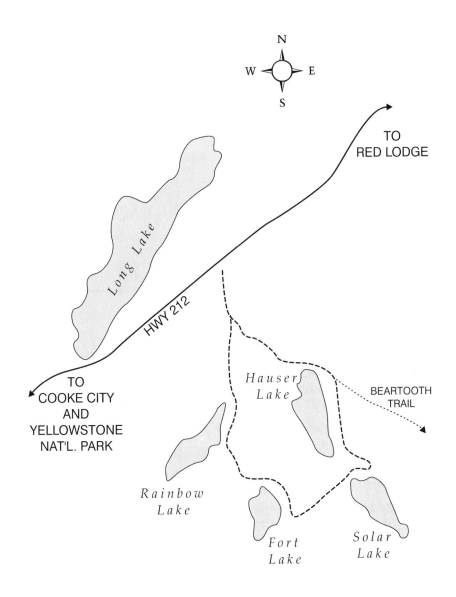

HAUSER, SOLAR, FORT AND RAINBOW LAKES

Red Lodge, Montana to Yellowstone National Park – **19**

Hike 7
Upper and Lower Chain Lakes

Hiking distance: 6 miles round trip
Hiking time: 4 hours
Elevation gain: 300 feet
Topo: R.M.S. Wyoming Beartooths
U.S.G.S. Beartooth Butte

Summary of hike: Located in the glacial terrain of the Beartooth Plateau, this hike follows a wide but seldom used jeep trail through an evergreen forest to open meadows. The meadows are marbled with streams, covered in wildflowers, and offer beautiful views, including a panoramic overview of Beartooth Butte.

Driving directions: Take Highway 212 to Long Lake, 36.5 miles from Red Lodge and 28 miles from Cooke City. Across the highway from the south end of Long Lake is a jeep trail. Park along the side of the jeep trail.

Hiking directions: Hike along the jeep trail to the bottom of the hill. The stream flows from Long Lake to Upper Chain Lake. You may stay on either the jeep trail that skirts the Chain Lakes or take the meadow to both lakes. Upper Chain Lake is about one mile from the trailhead, while Lower Chain Lake is just under two miles. Both lakes are visible from the trail. The jeep trail will continue past Dollar Lake on your left (2.2 miles) and Duck Lake on your right (3 miles). To return, follow the same trail back.

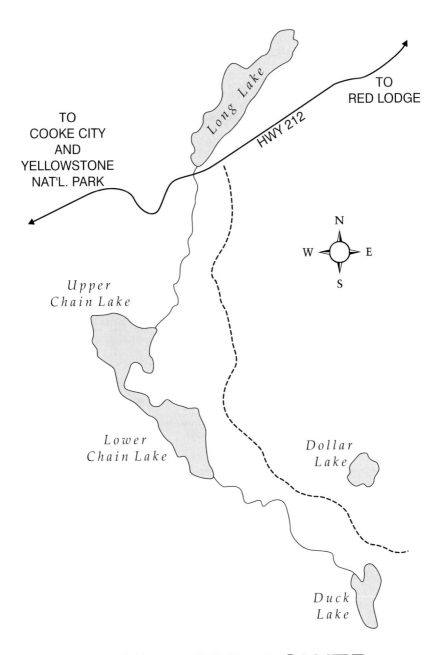

TO
COOKE CITY
AND
YELLOWSTONE
NAT'L. PARK

TO
RED LODGE

Long Lake

HWY 212

N
W   E
S

*Upper
Chain Lake*

*Lower
Chain Lake*

*Dollar
Lake*

*Duck
Lake*

UPPER AND LOWER
CHAIN LAKES

Hike 8
Dorf, Sheepherders, Snyder, Promise and Z Lakes

Hiking distance: 5.5 miles round trip
Hiking time: 3 hours
Elevation gain: 450 feet
Topo: R.M.S. Wyoming Beartooths
 U.S.G.S. Beartooth Butte

Summary of hike: This hike does not have a path. You walk along open meadows, following a stream from lake to lake. The meadows contain numerous streams that snake to the main drainage which feeds the various lakes. There are beautiful rocks covered with myriad colors of lichen. Evergreen trees break up the meadows and add to the variety of scenery.

Driving directions: Take Highway 212 to Long Lake, located 36.5 miles from Red Lodge and 28 miles from Cooke City. Just west of Long Lake is an unimproved road that heads north a short distance. Park anywhere along the side of the road and begin your hike.

Hiking directions: Walk north along the unimproved road a short distance. You will see a stream about 100 yards to your right. Cross the stream—using the rocks as stepping stones—and follow the stream uphill. The stream will lead you to Dorf Lake, a half mile from the trailhead. Lower and Upper Sheepherder Lakes are located about two miles from the trailhead. From Upper Sheepherder Lake, there are two hiking options. To the left, about 10 minutes away, is Snyder Lake. The other option is to continue northerly (uphill) to Lake Promise and Z Lake, located a half mile past Upper Sheepherder Lake. Each of these lakes are beautiful and worth the hike. Return along the same route by following the stream downhill.

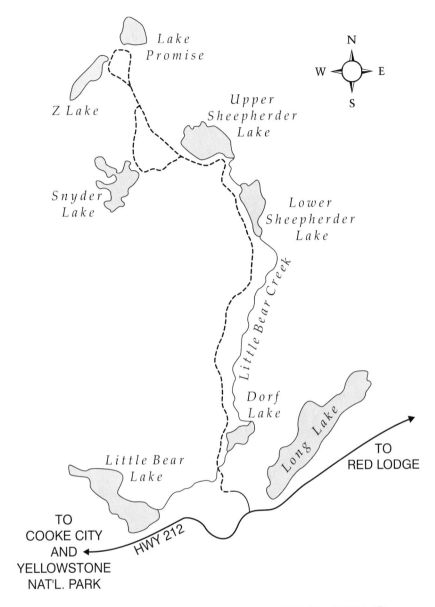

DORF, SHEEPHERDERS, SNYDER, PROMISE AND Z LAKES

Hike 9
Island & Night Lake

Hiking distance: 3 miles round trip
Hiking time: 1.5 hours
Elevation gain: Level hiking
Topo: R.M.S. Wyoming Beartooths
U.S.G.S. Beartooth Butte

Summary of hike: Located in the high lakes area of the Beartooths, this extremely scenic hike stays close to the west shore of both Island Lake and Night Lake (photo on page 30). Both lakes sit at an elevation of 9,500 feet. Island Lake, the larger of the two, encompasses more than 140 acres and contains several islands. There is a crossing of Little Bear Creek, guaranteeing some wet feet. This hike is the beginning portion of the Beartooth Highlakes Trail.

Driving directions: The trailhead is located 38 miles from Red Lodge and 26 miles from Cooke City on Highway 212. From the Island Lake turnoff, continue 0.4 miles to the trailhead parking area located near the boat launch.

Hiking directions: From the parking area, the trailhead is to the left towards the western shore of Island Lake. A short distance ahead, the trail meets Little Bear Creek, the outlet creek of Island Lake. Cross the creek and begin walking north along the shoreline. At the top of the lake, the trail continues by following the creek connecting the two lakes. Continue north, along the western shore of Night Lake. Although the trail continues farther into the backcountry, our turnaround spot is just north of Night Lake as the trail heads northwest, away from the creek. Return along the same path.

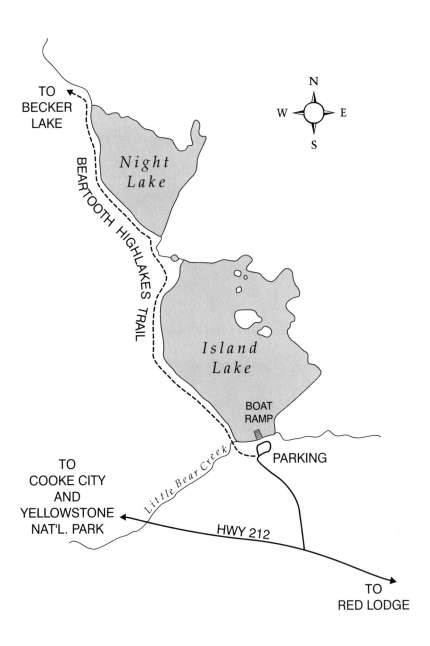

ISLAND AND NIGHT LAKES

Sheep Creek Falls - Hike 18

Long Lake - Hike 6

Lilies at Lily Lake - Hike 12

Pilot and Index Peaks - Hike 12

Hike 10
Beauty and Crane Lakes

Hiking distance: 4 miles round trip
Hiking time: 2 hours
Elevation gain: 520 feet
Topo: R.M.S. Wyoming Beartooths
U.S.G.S. Beartooth Butte

Summary of hike: The Beauty Lake Trail begins at Beartooth Lake, with the grandeur of Beartooth Butte towering 1,600 feet above the lake (photo on back cover). The trail passes through forests and alpine meadows at an elevation of more than 9,000 feet to Crane Lake and Beauty Lake. Both lakes are very picturesque. This hike is not recommended before mid-July, as Little Bear Creek can be dangerously high for crossing.

Driving directions: The turnoff to the trailhead is located 41.5 miles from downtown Red Lodge and 23 miles from Cooke City on Highway 212. Turn north at the Beartooth Lake Campground and drive 0.6 miles to the trailhead road. Turn left and continue 0.1 mile to the trailhead parking area.

Hiking directions: From the parking area, walk past the Forest Service sign along the trail towards Beartooth Lake. At 0.1 mile, take the right fork at the signed trail junction leading to the lakes. The trail crosses Little Bear Creek, which includes wet feet. The well-defined trail continues on the other side of the creek. At 1.3 miles, the trail passes the east shore of Crane Lake. Several spur trails lead down to the shore. The main trail follows the cascading creek upstream to the southern tip of Beauty Lake and parallels the eastern shore. This is our turn-around spot. To return, retrace your steps.

The Beauty Lake Trail intersects the Beartooth Highlakes Trail north of Beauty Lake. This is a popular hiking loop leading to Night and Island Lakes (Hike 9).

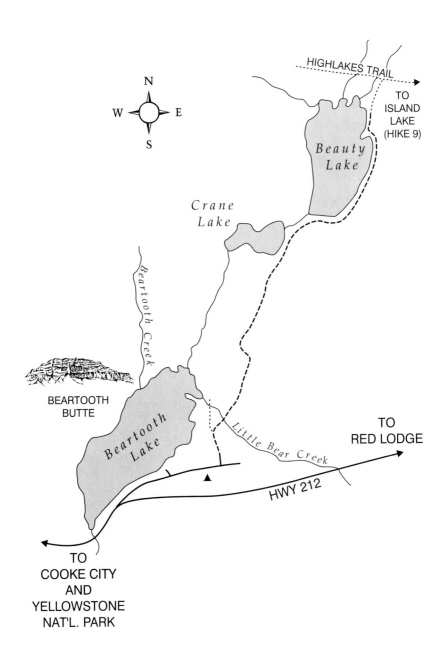

HIGHLAKES TRAIL

Beauty Lake

TO ISLAND LAKE (HIKE 9)

Crane Lake

Beartooth Creek

BEARTOOTH BUTTE

Beartooth Lake

Little Bear Creek

TO RED LODGE

HWY 212

TO COOKE CITY AND YELLOWSTONE NAT'L. PARK

N W E S

BEAUTY AND CRANE LAKES

Island Lake - Hike 9

Woody Falls - Hike 17

Bridal Falls - Hike 19

Wild Bill Lake - Hike 1

Hike 11
Beartooth Falls

Hiking distance: 1 mile round trip
Hiking time: 30 minutes
Elevation gain: 150 feet
Topo: R.M.S. Wyoming Beartooths
U.S.G.S. Beartooth Butte

Summary of hike: The trail to Beartooth Falls is not a designated trail. It is, however, a hike you will long remember. There is a short scramble over large rocks to one spectacular waterfall. A tremendous volume of water plunges over 100 feet.
CAUTION: You need to have good, stable footing while climbing over the rocks. The trail in this area is vague.

Driving directions: The trailhead is located 42 miles from downtown Red Lodge and 22.5 miles from Cooke City on Highway 212. There are several car pullouts on each side of the highway bridge crossing Beartooth Creek at the south end of Beartooth Lake.

Hiking directions: From the parking area, the trail begins to the west along the west side of Beartooth Creek. The trail heads south, following the creek downstream through the lush, green ground cover. Within ten minutes, the trail meets boulders on the right and Beartooth Creek on the left. Begin the climb up the boulders to the plateau at the top. The trail is not clearly defined, but all routes lead up to the same place. Once on top, follow a footpath down in the direction of the thunderous sound of the falls. There are various lookout spots, from the beginning cascades to the lookout atop the falls. The views are guaranteed to give you vertigo. After admiring this powerful display of water, return along the same route.

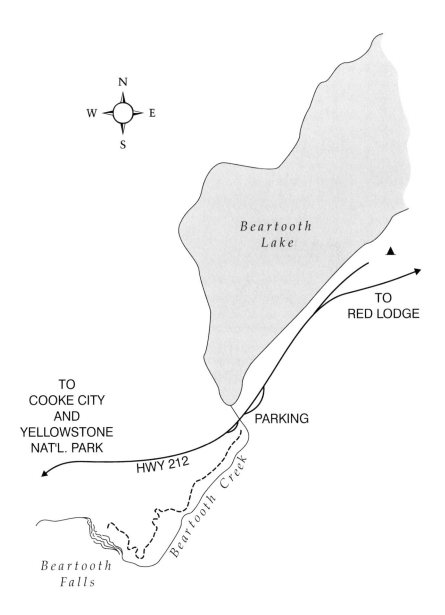

N
W   E
S

Beartooth
Lake

TO
RED LODGE

TO
COOKE CITY
AND
YELLOWSTONE
NAT'L. PARK

PARKING

HWY 212

Beartooth Creek

Beartooth
Falls

BEARTOOTH FALLS

Red Lodge, Montana to Yellowstone National Park – **33**

Hike 12
Lily Lake

Hiking distance: 1 mile loop
Hiking time: 30 minutes
Elevation gain: 100 feet
Topo: R.M.S. Wyoming Beartooths
U.S.G.S. Muddy Creek

Summary of hike: This hike is a one-mile loop along the southern portion of Lily Lake, which has an abundance of water lilies and is surrounded by a forest. This beautiful, 40-acre mountain lake sits at 7,670 feet. Some of the best views of Pilot and Index Peak can be seen along the Lily Lake Road enroute to the lake (photos on page 27).

Driving directions: The turnoff to the trailhead is located 50 miles from downtown Red Lodge and 14.5 miles from Cooke City on Highway 212. Turn north from Highway 212 onto Lily Lake Road. Drive up the winding road 1.2 miles to the T-junction. Turn right and continue 0.5 miles towards Lily Lake. As you approach the campground, turn right at each of the first two road forks. Park at the end of the road by the campsites.

Hiking directions: From the parking area, the unmarked trailhead begins to the left. Cross the Lake Creek tributary using stepping stones. The trail leads through the forest to the shoreline of Lily Lake near a rock outcropping. Take the fisherman trail to the left, which borders the lake along the southwest shore. Continue to the boat launch area. Walk up the gravel road leading back to the parking area on the left.

If you wish to hike further, there are additional trails along the lake north of the boat launch.

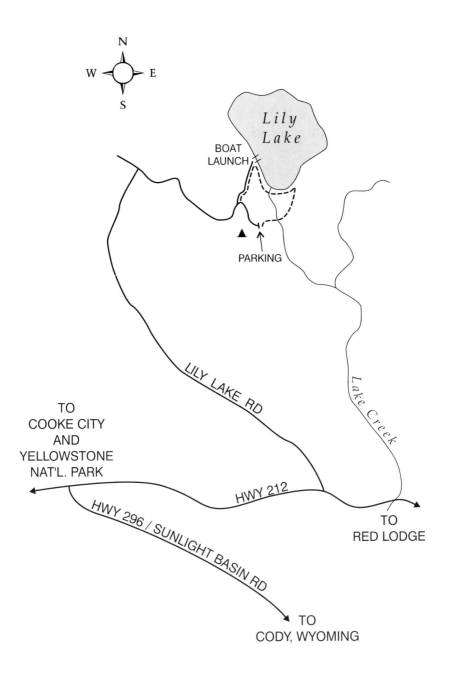

LILY LAKE

Hike 13
Crazy Creek Falls

Hiking distance: 1 mile round trip
Hiking time: 1/2 hour
Elevation gain: 150 feet
Topo: R.M.S. Wyoming Beartooths
U.S.G.S. Jim Smith Peak

Summary of hike: This hike is different from the other hikes in the book. In a short 15 minutes, you are at the destination spot, but it is worth spending the day. There are flat, terraced rocks for sunbathing or hiking around, cascading waters and waterfalls, soaking pools, and even a bubble-filled "Jacuzzi." This natural water park is a favorite spot for those who know about it.

Driving directions: The trailhead is located 53 miles from Red Lodge or 11 miles from Cooke City on Highway 212. Pull into the parking turnout on the north, directly across from the Crazy Creek Campground.

Hiking directions: From the parking turnout, follow the Crazy Creek Lakes Trail. After five to ten minutes, watch on the left for a large, flat terrace of rocks. Leave the trail and hike along this terrace toward the sound of the water. This will quickly lead you to the water playground.

Use caution in this area as the rocks can be slick and the water swift.

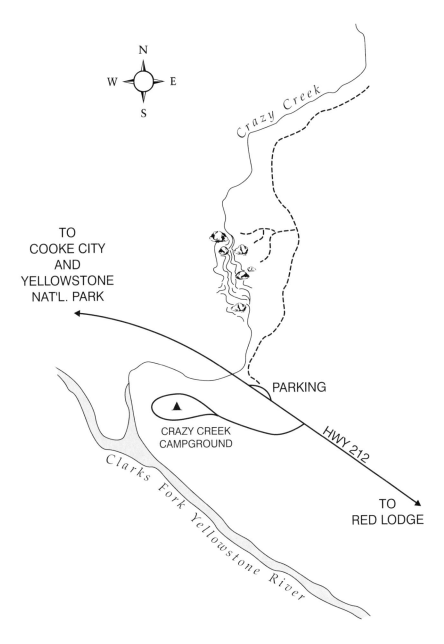

CRAZY CREEK

Hike 14
Lillis and Vernon Lakes

Hiking distance: 5.5 miles
Hiking time: 3 hours
Elevation gain: 600 feet
Topo: R.M.S. Cooke City
U.S.G.S. Fossil Lake

Summary of hike: Lillis and Vernon Lakes are located in the Absaroka-Beartooth Wilderness. This is a real backcountry wilderness hike. Few people hike to these lakes, so chances are you will not see anyone along the trail. You may spot moose, which frequent the meadows. Lillis Lake is surrounded by dense forest and mountains peaks, including Pilot and Index Peaks looming above. Mosquito repellent is highly recommended in the early summer.

Driving directions: The trailhead is located 61 miles from downtown Red Lodge and 3.5 miles from Cooke City on Highway 212. It is directly across the highway from Chief Joseph Campground. A trailhead sign posted along the highway reads "Clarks Fork Trailhead." Turn here and park in the parking lot 0.2 miles ahead.

Hiking directions: From the parking area, take the Kersey Lake Trail towards the bridge over the Clarks Fork (cover photo). The Clarks Fork Canyon Falls is 100 feet downstream from the bridge. After crossing the bridge, continue 1.2 miles, parallel to Sedge Creek, to the posted trail junction to Vernon Lake. The trail climbs gently, then heads down to a boggy area. Logs are placed in this area to be used as walking aids. The trail quickly drops down to Lillis Lake. To hike further, continue following the northwest shore of Lillis Lake as the trail descends 300 feet through a dense forest to Vernon Lake. The trail ends at the north shore of the lake. Return along the same trail.

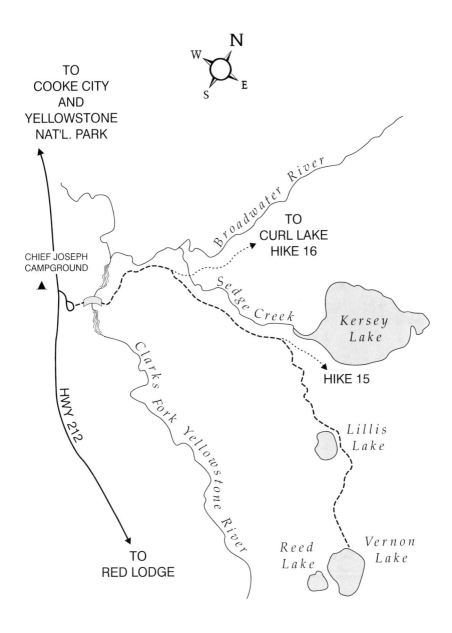

LILLIS AND VERNON LAKES

Red Lodge, Montana to Yellowstone National Park – **39**

Hike 15
Kersey Lake

Hiking distance: 3 miles round trip
Hiking time: 1.5 hours
Elevation gain: 100 feet
Topo: R.M.S. Cooke City
 U.S.G.S. Fossil Lake

Summary of hike: Kersey Lake is a large alpine lake surrounded by a rocky shore and forest. The trail to the lake follows the Broadwater River upstream for the first portion of the hike. The remainder of the trail parallels Sedge Creek, the outlet creek from Kersey Lake. This forested hike is easy and gains little elevation. Near the trailhead is the Clarks Fork Canyon Falls and a magnificent cascade.

Driving directions: The trailhead is located 61 miles from Red Lodge and 3.5 miles from Cooke City on Highway 212. It is directly across the highway from Chief Joseph Campground. A trailhead sign along the highway reads "Clarks Fork Trailhead." Turn here and park in the parking lot 0.2 miles ahead.

Hiking directions: From the trailhead, walk to the bridge crossing the cascading Clarks Fork (cover photo). There are two well-defined trails—a horse pack trail and a foot trail—that lead to Kersey Lake. At 0.5 miles, you will pass a trail junction on the left that follows along the Broadwater River to Curl and Broadwater Lakes (Hike 16). Stay on the main trail to Kersey Lake. At 1.2 miles is another trail junction on the right leading to Vernon Lake (Hike 14). Stay on the main trail. Near Kersey Lake is another trail junction on the right to Rock Island Lake. Again, stay on the main trail, which is minutes away from the south shore of Kersey Lake. The lake is our turnaround spot.

   If you wish to hike further, the trail to Rock Island Lake parallels the south shore of Kersey Lake.

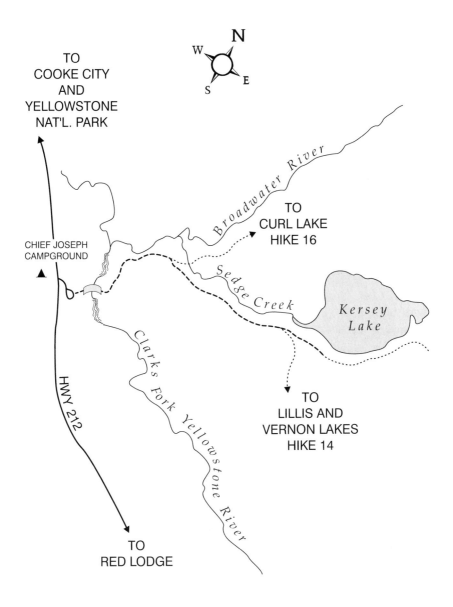

KERSEY LAKE

Hike 16
Broadwater River to Curl Lake

Hiking distance: 6.5 miles round trip
Hiking time: 3.5 hours
Elevation gain: 250 feet
Topo: R.M.S. Cooke City
U.S.G.S. Fossil Lake

Summary of hike: This hike takes you to an area where you feel like you're on top of the world. It leads past cascading water, open meadows, and trees to majestic high country lakes. Part of this hike goes through the burn area from the 1988 Yellowstone fires.

Driving directions: The trailhead is located 61 miles from Red Lodge and 3.5 miles from Cooke City on Highway 212. It is directly across the highway from Chief Joseph Campground. A trailhead sign along Highway 212 reads "Clarks Fork Trailhead." Turn here and park in the parking lot 0.2 miles ahead.

Hiking directions: The hike begins at the north end of the parking lot near the cascade and waterfall. The Clarks Fork Canyon Falls is 100 feet downstream from the wooden bridge. Follow the trail over the bridge (cover photo). At 0.5 miles, watch for a wooden "Broadwater River Trail" sign to the left. Take this trail to the left. Continue gently uphill another 0.5 miles to a second posted trail junction, which reads "Broadwater River Trail." Stay on this trail, following the cascading water upstream to Curl Lake. Curl Lake is three miles from the trailhead. The trail parallels the east shoreline of the lake. To return, retrace your steps.

If you would like to extend your hike another half mile, continue hiking to Broadwater Lake.

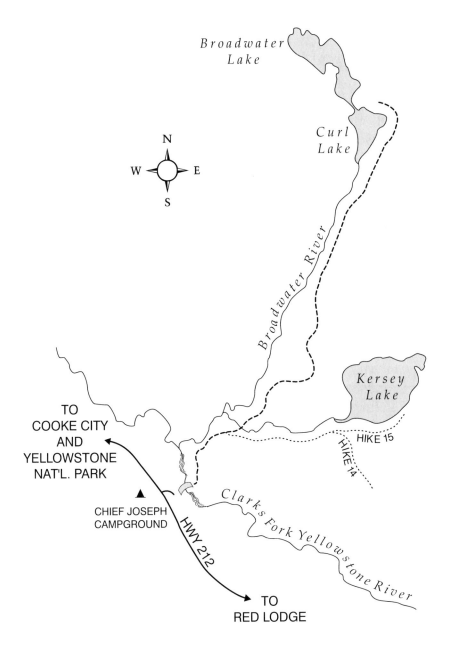

BROADWATER RIVER
TO CURL LAKE

Hike 17
Woody Falls

Hiking distance: 3 miles round trip
Hiking time: 1:45 hours
Elevation gain: 700 feet
Topo: R.M.S. Cooke City
U.S.G.S. Cooke City

Summary of hike: Woody Falls is a spectacular 150-foot, three-tier falls with a pool at the base (photo on page 30). The falls is a popular destination for the locals as well as a cross-country ski trail in the winter. The trailhead is located in the heart of downtown Cooke City. The hike begins on an old mining road that leads to Mohawk Mine.

Driving directions: From downtown Cooke City, no driving is required. The trailhead is located by the old general store on the corner of Highway 212 and River Street. Head south on River Street a half block to the buck fence trail entrance.

Hiking directions: From the buck fence, walk south on the trail, passing old log cabins. Cross the wooden footbridge over Soda Butte Creek. Continue straight ahead up the jeep trail. Within five minutes from the trailhead is a well-defined footpath on the left. This is the trail to Woody Falls. As a short side trip, stay on the jeep road an additional 200 yards, just past a tree with a sign reading "Woody Creek Ski Trail." Take the spur trail to the right 300 feet more to a beautiful cascade and smaller waterfall. After viewing the falls, return to the main jeep trail and the Woody Falls Trail. The well-worn footpath begins a steady uphill climb through the forest. As the canyon below narrows, you will hear the sound of the falls on your right. Spur trails lead to the canyon edge for a variety of commanding overviews of Woody Falls. Return along the same trail.

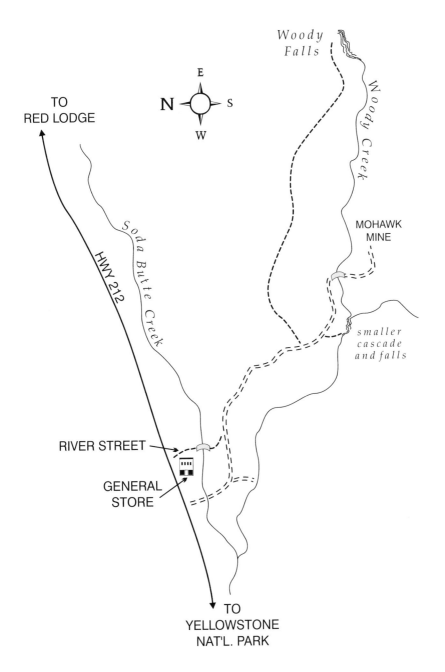

WOODY FALLS

Hike 18
Sheep Creek Falls

Hiking distance: 0.6 miles round trip
Hiking time: 20 minutes
Elevation gain: 200 feet
Topo: R.M.S. Cooke City
      U.S.G.S. Cooke City

Summary of hike: Sheep Creek Falls is a magnificent, full-bodied waterfall (photo on page 26). Although it is only 0.3 miles to the falls, it is not an easy hike. It is more of a scramble over timber, up the canyon along Sheep Creek. There is no defined trail, and it is not recommended for children. The hike climbs through a burn area from the 1988 Yellowstone fires.

Driving directions: The trailhead is located 1.1 miles west of Cooke City and 1.6 miles east of Silver Gate. The parking pullout is located on the south side of the highway and the west side of the Sheep Creek bridge.

Hiking directions: From the parking pullout, cross to the north side of Highway 212. Walk upstream along the east side of Sheep Creek. The trail fades in and out. Just scramble up, climbing over and around the down trees, using Sheep Creek as your guide. At a quarter mile, the canyon curves to the right. From this spot, the magnificence of Sheep Falls is directly in front of you. Return by heading back downstream to the highway.

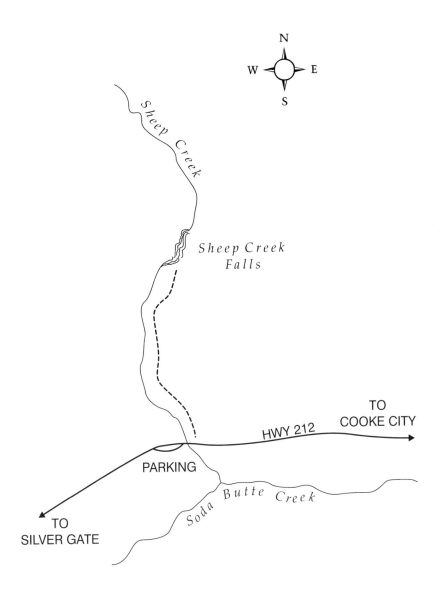

SHEEP CREEK FALLS

Hike 19
Bridal Falls

Hiking distance: 0.6 miles round trip
Hiking time: 15 minutes
Elevation gain: 50 feet
Topo: R.M.S. Cooke City
          U.S.G.S. Cooke City

Summary of hike: Bridal Falls, unofficially named, drops out of steep granite cliffs to a ledge. From the ledge, the water shoots out horizontal, dropping more than forty additional feet into a pool (photo on page 31). Ferns and moss grow along these sheer rock walls. The trail is a short and easy path that parallels Wyoming Creek through the forest.

Driving directions: From downtown Silver Gate, turn south from Highway 212 onto Monument Avenue. Drive 0.2 miles to the end of the road. Turn left on Bannock Trail and continue 0.8 miles to the Wyoming Creek bridge, the only bridge along the road. Park off road before crossing the bridge.

Hiking directions: From the road, walk upstream along the west side of Wyoming Creek. The path leads south for 0.3 miles to the base of the falls and pool. The mountain on the left (east) of the falls is Republic Mountain. To the right (west) is Wall Rock. Return along the same trail.

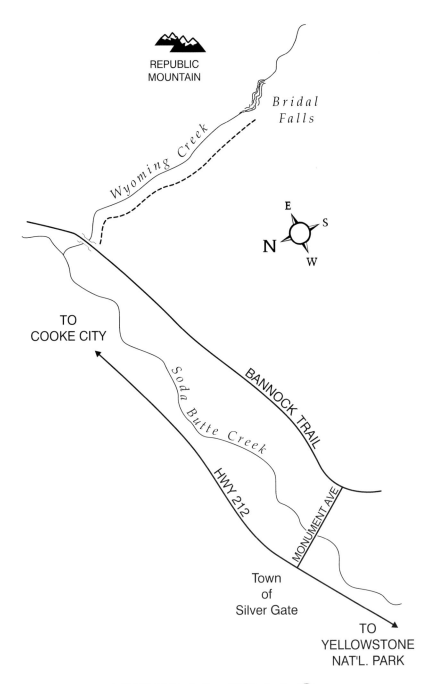

BRIDAL FALLS

Hike 20
Silver Falls

Hiking distance: 2 miles round trip
Hiking time: 1 hour
Elevation gain: 350 feet
Topo: R.M.S. Cooke City
U.S.G.S. Cooke City

Summary of hike: Silver Falls is a narrow but long waterfall with a drop of more than 100 feet. The hike to the falls is located along the eastern border of Yellowstone National Park. There is no trail to the falls. It is a scramble over and around down trees, parallel to Silver Creek. The terrain is rough and not recommended for children.

Driving directions: The trailhead is located 0.6 miles west of Silver Gate, just outside the border of Yellowstone National Park. Watch for Silver Creek on the north side of the road. Pull into an old road west of the creek and park. You may also park about 100 yards ahead in a car pullout on the north side of the road by the Yellowstone National Park border sign.

Hiking directions: From either parking area, walk back to Silver Creek. Follow the creek upstream along the west side of the creek. There is no trail, and there are many down trees to navigate around. Continue to follow the creek, which leads to the falls. The last quarter mile is a steep climb up a knoll, leaving the creek below. At the top is a view across the canyon of Silver Falls.

There is also a second route to view the falls. Instead of climbing the knoll, stay close to Silver Creek in the canyon. This route will take you to the base of the falls.

From either route, return by following the creek downstream.

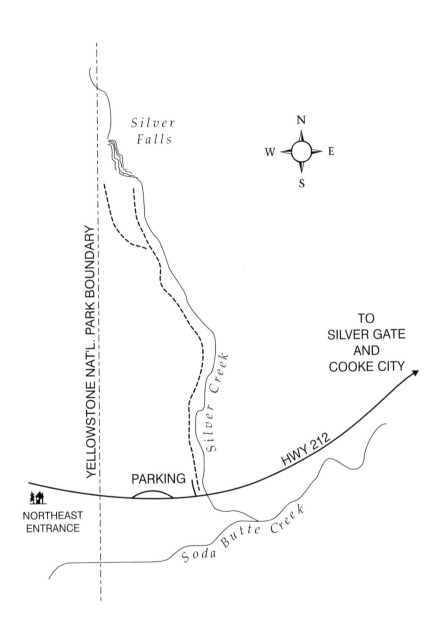

Silver Falls

YELLOWSTONE NAT'L. PARK BOUNDARY

Silver Creek

TO
SILVER GATE
AND
COOKE CITY

HWY 212

PARKING

NORTHEAST
ENTRANCE

Soda Butte Creek

N
W E
S

SILVER FALLS

Notes

Information Sources

Gallatin National Forest
3710 Sallon St.
Bozeman, MT 59715
(406) 587-6920
(406) 587-6701

Shoshone National Forest
808 Meadow Lane
Cody, WY 82414
(307) 527-6241

Custer National Forest
2602 1st. Ave. North
P.O. Box 2556
Billings, MT 59103
(406) 657-6361

Beartooth Ranger District
Custer National Forest
P.O. Box 3420
Red Lodge, MT 59068
(406) 446-2103

Montana Fish, Wildlife & Parks
1420 E. 6th. Ave.
Helena, MT 59620
(406) 444-2535
In Billings: (406) 252-4654
              (406) 252-4655

Wyoming Game and Fish
5400 Bishop Blvd.
Cheyenne, WY 82006
(307) 777-4600

Travel Montana
Montana Dept. of Commerce
P.O. Box 200533
Helena, MT 59620
(406) 444-2654
(800) 541-1447
outside Montana (800) 847-4868

Wyoming Dept. of Tourism
I-25 and College Dr.
Cheyenne, WY 82002
(800) 225-5996

Yellowstone Country Tourism
P.O. Box 1107
Red Lodge, MT 59068
(800) 736-5276
(406) 446-1005

Yellowstone National Park
P.O. Box 168
Y.N.P., WY 82190
(307) 344-7381

Red Lodge Area
  Chamber of Commerce
P.O. Box 988
Red Lodge, MT 59068
(406) 446-1718

Cody, Wyoming
Chamber of Commerce
(307) 587-8585

Cooke City and Silver Gate, MT
Chamber of Commerce
(406) 838-2272

Greater Yellowstone Coalition
P.O. Box 1874
Bozeman, MT 59771
(406) 586-1593

Hamilton Stores Inc.
1709 W. College St.
Bozeman, MT 59715
(406) 587-2208   646-7325

Yellowstone Institute
P.O. Box 117
Y.N.P, WY 82190
(307) 344-7381   ext. 2349
(307) 344-2294   in Mammoth
(307) 344-7749   in Lamar Valley

TW Recreational Services
Lodging Reservations
(307) 344-7311

Yellowstone Camping
(307) 344-2114

Other Day Hike Guidebooks

___ Day Hikes on Oahu $6.95
___ Day Hikes on Maui.................................... 8.95
___ Day Hikes on Kauai.................................. 8.95
___ Day Trips on St. Martin............................. 9.95
___ Day Hikes in Denver 6.95
___ Day Hikes in Boulder, Colorado 8.95
___ Day Hikes in Steamboat Springs, Colorado............ 8.95
___ Day Hikes in Summit County, Colorado 8.95
___ Day Hikes in Aspen, Colorado 7.95
___ Day Hikes in Yosemite National Park
    25 Favorite Hikes 8.95
___ Day Hikes Around Lake Tahoe 8.95
___ Day Hikes in Yellowstone National Park
    25 Favorite Hikes 7.95
___ Day Hikes in the Grand Tetons and Jackson Hole, WY.... 7.95
___ Day Hikes in Los Angeles
    Malibu to Hollywood 8.95
___ Day Hikes in the Beartooth Mountains
    Red Lodge, Montana to Yellowstone National Park 8.95

These books may be purchased at your local bookstore or they will be glad to order them. For a full list of titles available directly from ICS Books, call toll-free 1-800-541-7323. Visa or Mastercard accepted.

- -

Please include $2.00 per order to cover postage and handling. Please send the books marked above. I enclose $ _____

Name _____

Address _____

City _____ State _____ Zip _____

Credit Card # _____ Exp. _____

Signature _____

1-800-541-7323

Distributed by:
ICS Books, Inc.
1370 E. 86th Place, Merrillville, In. 46410
1-800-541-7323 · Fax 1-800-336-8334

TOM EGENES

About the Author

The lure of the beautiful Rocky Mountains drew Robert to Red Lodge, Montana, in 1979. Hiking, horsepacking, and living in the Rockies has fulfilled a lifelong dream.

Robert Stone has traveled and photographed extensively throughout Asia, Europe, the Caribbean, Hawaii, and the Continental United States.